Beginner's Guide to
Mod Podge®

Welcome to fast and easy decoupage! This handy guide introduces the versatile line of Mod Podge® products and explains how to use them to create unique home accessories and crafts.

For more project ideas and inspiration, visit www.plaidonline.com

D1584792

LEISURE ARTS, INC. • Maumelle, Arkansas

Mod Podge® Products

Decoupage is simply the art of cut-and-paste, used with paper or fabric cut-outs to decorate virtually any surface. Decoupage was all the rage in the 60's, but quite tedious, requiring layers of varnish and sanding. In 1967, decoupage devotee Jan Wetstone invented a fast and easy alternative: Mod Podge, a takeoff on modern decoupage. It's ideal for: home décor, gifts, upcycling, kids' crafts, mixed media, and more.

Mod Podge is a brushable medium that works beautifully when adhering paper and/or fabric to almost any surface. It also works as a sealer and finish. As it is brushed over a project surface it appears milky white when wet, yet dries quickly to a clear, durable finish that seals and protects. The time-tested waterbase, non-toxic formula is manufactured near Atlanta, GA by Plaid Enterprises, Inc., a leading manufacturer of craft and home décor products.

Which Mod Podge® Should I Use?

	canvas	fabric	glass & ceramics	home decorating	holiday projects	jewelry	kids' projects	paper	papier-mâché	plastic/plexi/vinyl	scrapbooking	special effects	styrofoam	wood	metal
Classic Gloss	•	•	•	•	•	•	•	•	•	•	•		•	•	•
Classic Matte	•	•	•	•	•	•	•	•	•	•	•		•	•	•
Satin	•	•	•	•	•		•						•	•	•
Ultra Matte Chalk	•	•	•	•	•	•	•	•	•	•	•	•		•	•
Fabric		•		•	•		•	•							
Outdoor	•	•	•	•	•		•	•	•	•			•	•	•
Furniture	•	•	•	•	•		•	•	•	•			•	•	•
Dishwasher Safe	•		•	•				•						•	•
Paper Matte & Gloss								•	•		•				
Super Gloss			•	•	•	•	•	•	•	•		•		•	•
Sparkle	•	•	•	•	•	•	•	•	•	•	•	•	•	•	•
Stiffy		•													
Dimensional Magic				•		•		•	•		•	•		•	•

Classic Mod Podge (Matte & Gloss)
The original Mod Podge formulas. Matte will give your project a non-shiny finish, and the Gloss formula will offer a shiny finish when dry.

Mod Podge Satin
This formula will give your projects a smooth, soft-to-the-touch satiny finish.

Mod Podge Fabric
The best for fabric-to-fabric decoupage. Perfect for wearables, accessories, linens, and more. Hand wash as needed.

Mod Podge Ultra Matte Chalk
Trend right Ultra Matte chalk finish brushes on smoothly without visible brushstrokes.

Mod Podge Outdoor
Rain or shine, appliqued and painted decoupage projects maintain their beauty for outdoor living. Use on tin, wood, terra cotta, slate, and more.

Mod Podge Paper Matte
Exceptional for card crafts, scrapbooks, altered art, and any paper-to-paper project. Also available in Gloss.

Mod Podge Furniture Satin
Give your most frequently used projects an extra durable finish with Mod Podge Furniture. Perfect for furniture, bookshelves, kitchen accessories, and more. Also available in Matte and Gloss.

Mod Podge Super Gloss
Provides an extra-thick, glass-like finish in one coat, without visible brush strokes. Ultra clear and ultra dramatic.

Mod Podge Sparkle
Add extra glitter and sparkle to your projects. Apply multiple coats to achieve extra glitz and glamour.

Mod Podge Stiffy
Add dimension to your craft projects with Stiffy®, the original fabric stiffener. This classic medium is perfect for stiffening fabric, ribbon, lace, needlework, and more.

Mod Podge Dishwasher Safe
Your projects are easier to clean with the top-rack dishwasher safe formula. Perfect for glass, ceramics, and metals.

Mod Podge Dimensional Magic
Add clear dramatic dimension to your projects. The stay-put formula adds epoxy-like accents and texture, creating mosaic, quilt, and other effects.

BASICS

Be sure to read and familiarize yourself with the information on pages 2-5 before beginning your project.

Basic Tools

Mod Podge Silicone Craft Mat • scissors • craft knife pencil • ruler • tape measure • squeegee • brayer assorted sizes of bristle and foam brushes • brush basin sandpaper • paper towels • tack cloth

Preparing the Surface to Be Decoupaged

Almost any surface can be decoupaged with Mod Podge; the prep work is simple.

Wood: Lightly sand and wipe away the sanding dust with a slightly damp paper towel or tack cloth. If directed, apply 2 coats of acrylic paint, allowing to dry and sand between coats.

Glass: Wash in warm soapy water; rinse with warm water and dry. Wipe with rubbing alcohol to remove any soap residue or skin oils.

Papier-Mâché: Wipe with a slightly damp paper towel.

Fabric: Wash and dry the fabrics; do not use fabric softener, dryer sheets, or spray starch. Press the fabrics smooth.

Metal: Wash in warm soapy water; rinse with warm water and dry. Wipe with white vinegar.

Plastic: Wash in warm soapy water; rinse with warm water and dry. Mod Podge may not adhere to all plastics; be sure to test for good adhesion on a small area.

Applying Mod Podge

Always work on a covered work surface for fast clean-up and to protect the work surface.

Paper to Wood:

- Cut the paper(s) to the exact size to fit the project. It is easier to cut it now than later.

- If paper is thin, such as photocopy/printer paper, let the ink dry for 10 minutes after printing. Apply several light coats of Mod Podge Clear Acrylic Sealer to both sides of the paper.

- If paper is thick, such as scrapbook paper or cardstock, or was printed on a laser printer, no preparation is necessary.

- Apply a medium coat (the product is white and visible on the surface) of Mod Podge to the wood surface *(Photo 1)* and the back of the paper. Too little glue will cause wrinkles; you can always wipe away any excess glue.

- Place the paper on the wood and smooth with a brayer or squeegee from the center towards the edges *(Photo 2)*. Remove excess with a slightly damp paper towel. Keep smoothing with the tool until the paper is smooth.

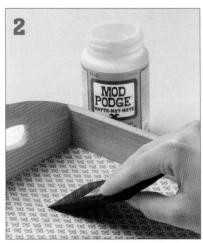

- Let Mod Podge dry for 15-20 minutes. Apply 2-3 light protective coats of Mod Podge to the entire surface, allowing to dry between each coat *(Photo 3)*.

- Glossy finishes may remain tacky after drying. Spray the surface with Mod Podge Acrylic Sealer.

Paper to Glass:
- Follow the same application instructions as for Paper to Wood, page 4.

Paper to Paper (including Papier-Mâché)
- Follow the same application instructions as for Paper to Wood, page 4.

Fabric to Fabric:
- Apply a thin coat of Mod Podge to the wrong side of the fabrics that will be cut and decoupaged. Allow to dry. This gives the fabrics body and prevents fraying. Once dry, cut the fabrics as instructed.

- Apply a light coat of Mod Podge to the wrong side of the fabric piece to be decoupaged. Place the fabric appliqué on the fabric background and smooth with a brayer or squeegee. Keep smoothing with the tool until the fabric is smooth.

- Let the Mod Podge dry for 20-30 minutes. Apply 2-3 light protective coats of Mod Podge to the surface, allowing to dry between each coat.

Paper to Metal:
- Follow the same application instructions as for Paper to Wood, page 4.

TIPS

Here are a few tips to make crafting with Mod Podge even more fun.

- A 1-inch flat paintbrush is great for applying Mod Podge. Be sure to wash the brush immediately after use. When applying the protective topcoats of Mod Podge, you may wish to use a 1-inch foam brush with light pressure to minimize the appearance of brushstrokes.

- Dip your brush in clean water then blot the excess before you dip it in the Mod Podge for the first time. This softens the brush and allows the Mod Podge to flow smoothly.

- A brayer or squeegee tool is essential for smoothing the paper or fabric on your project. A squeegee works for those tight corners and other small areas/spaces.

See The USA Boxes

SHOPPING LIST

- ☐ Mod Podge® Satin
- ☐ FolkArt® Home Decor Chalk™ (Nantucket Blue)
- ☐ Assorted map-themed & woodgrain scrapbook paper
- ☐ Assorted travel-related stickers & paper motifs
- ☐ Round papier-mâché boxes (ours measure 4", $3^1/_2$", & $2^3/_4$" high)

- ☐ 3 assorted wooden knobs
- ☐ 3 assorted bases (we used a china egg cup, a wooden candlestick & a glass candlestick)
- ☐ E6000® Industrial Strength Adhesive
- ☐ Basic tools

Before beginning your project, be sure to read & familiarize yourself with the information on pages 2-5.

To make each Box:
Always allow paint and Mod Podge to dry completely between applications.

1. With the lid on the box, measure the height (from the bottom edge of the lid to the bottom of the box) and the circumference of your box. Add $^1/_2$" to the circumference measurement. Cut a piece of map-themed paper these measurements, piecing if needed.

2. Measure the height of the lid and cut a piece of woodgrain paper this measurement by the circumference, piecing if needed. Turn the lid upside down and draw around it on the woodgrain paper; cut out on drawn line.

3. Use Mod Podge to adhere the paper to the box and use the squeegee to smooth the paper. Repeat with the lid top and sides.

4. Cut the desired phrases and motifs from scrapbook paper. Use Mod Podge to adhere them to the box. Add stickers to the box, if using. Apply 2-3 topcoats of Mod Podge to the box and lid.

5. Apply 2 coats of Nantucket Blue to the base. For a weathered look, lightly sand the base.

6. Use the E6000® Adhesive to attach the base and the knob to the box.

Favorite Things Tray

SHOPPING LIST

- ☐ Mod Podge® Super Gloss
- ☐ Mod Podge® Matte
- ☐ FolkArt® Home Decor Chalk™ (Savannah & Turkish Tile)
- ☐ Assorted scrapbook papers
- ☐ Assorted phrases, motifs & small strips cut from paper
- ☐ Wooden tray (our tray is 9" x 14")
- ☐ Basic tools

Before beginning your project, be sure to read & familiarize yourself with the information on pages 2-5.

To make the Tray:

Always allow paint and Mod Podge to dry completely between applications.

1. Prepare the tray. Paint the tray with Savannah. Paint the tray with Turkish Tile. When dry, lightly sand the edges to allow some of the Savannah to show through to create a distressed look.

2. Arrange 2-3 large background pieces of scrapbook paper, the phrases, motifs, and strips in the tray until you are pleased with the look. **Tip:** Take a photo or make a rough sketch of the arrangement. Remove all the paper pieces.

3. Working from the background up, use Mod Podge Matte to adhere the paper pieces to the tray. Use the squeegee or brayer to smooth the paper.

4. Slowly pour Mod Podge Super Gloss in the tray. Use the brush to spread the Mod Podge over the entire tray bottom with as few brushstrokes as possible. Allow the Mod Podge to settle and smooth out.

Washer Necklaces

SHOPPING LIST

- ☐ Mod Podge® Dimensional Magic
- ☐ Mod Podge® Matte
- ☐ Metal washers (we used 2-3 $1/2$"- $1^3/8$" dia. washers per necklace)
- ☐ Scrapbook paper scraps
- ☐ Pre-made leather cord necklaces
- ☐ Basic tools

Before beginning your project, be sure to read & familiarize yourself with the information on pages 2-5.

To make each Necklace:

1. Draw around each washer on the wrong side of scrapbook paper, being sure to draw around the inner circle also; cut out on drawn lines.

2. Apply a coat of Mod Podge Matte to the wrong side of the paper circles and to the surface of the washers. Firmly press each circle onto its corresponding washer; allow to dry.

3. Place the washers, paper side up, on your work surface. Apply a coat of Dimensional Magic over the paper and allow to dry (*Photo 1*).

4. Apply a coat of Dimensional Magic to the back of the washers and allow to dry.

5. Thread the washers on the necklace.

Out Of This World Letter

SHOPPING LIST

- ☐ Mod Podge® Matte
- ☐ 12" x 12" sheet of space-themed scrapbook paper
- ☐ 3 pieces of coordinating scrapbook paper
- ☐ Chipboard letter with a flat surface (ours measures 13" high)
- ☐ 2 wooden stars (we used $3^1/_2$" & $2^1/_2$" high stars)
- ☐ Wooden circle (we used a 3" dia. circle)
- ☐ Silver chenille stem
- ☐ Adhesive-backed foam dots
- ☐ Craft glue
- ☐ Basic tools

Before beginning your project, be sure to read & familiarize yourself with the information on pages 2-5.

To make the Letter:

Always allow Mod Podge to dry completely between applications.

1. Decide which areas of your letter will have space-themed paper and which will be coordinating paper. Place the letter face down on the wrong side of the space-themed piece of scrapbook paper; draw around the letter. Repeat to draw around the stars, circle, and any letter accent areas on the coordinating papers. Cut out shapes on the drawn lines.

2. Apply Mod Podge to the wrong side of the paper letter and to the surface of the chipboard letter. Carefully place the paper letter on the chipboard letter. Use the squeegee or brayer to smooth the paper. Repeat with the stars, circle, and accent shapes.

3. Apply 2-3 topcoats of Mod Podge to each shape.

4. Use foam dots to adhere the shapes to the letter.

5. Trimming as needed, glue the chenille stem around the circle.

Maps & Flowers Table

SHOPPING LIST

☐ Mod Podge® Furniture Satin

☐ FolkArt® Home Decor Chalk™ (we used Willow Mist & Castle)

☐ Small side table (our table top is 12" x 12" and the table is 22¹/₂" high)

☐ Scrapbook paper (we used vintage map, polka dot, & floral papers)

☐ Basic tools

Before beginning your project, be sure to read & familiarize yourself with the information on pages 2-5.

To make the Table:

Always allow paint and Mod Podge to dry completely between applications.

1. Paint the entire table with Willow Mist. Paint the entire table with Castle. When dry, lightly sand the table to allow some Willow Mist to show through for a distressed look.

2. Measure your table top and piecing if needed, cut your background papers to fit (we used the map-themed and polka dot papers for the background). Cut the desired motifs from accent paper (we used the floral for the accents).

3. Apply Mod Podge to the wrong side of the background paper and the table top. Position the background paper on the table top. Use the squeegee or brayer to smooth the paper.

4. Use Mod Podge to adhere the motifs to the table top.

5. Apply 2-3 topcoats of Mod Podge to the entire table top.

Home Sweet Home Tote Bag

SHOPPING LIST

☐ Mod Podge® Fabric

☐ Assorted fabric scraps (we used 6 different fabrics)

☐ Canvas tote bag (ours is 13" x 13$\frac{1}{2}$" x 3")

☐ Tracing paper

☐ Basic tools

Before beginning your project, be sure to read & familiarize yourself with the information on pages 2-5.

To make the Tote Bag:

1. Decide the desired fabric combinations for each house.

2. Trace the patterns, page 31, onto tracing paper and cut out.

3. Roughly draw around each pattern (about $\frac{1}{2}$" larger) on the *wrong* side of the corresponding fabric piece; repeat to draw a total of 3 of each pattern. Apply Mod Podge in the marked areas and allow to dry completely.

4. Center a pattern in the corresponding marked area; draw around the pattern and cut out on the drawn line. Repeat to make a total of 3 fabric shapes from each pattern. Arrange the shapes as desired on the tote bag.

5. Use Mod Podge to adhere the fabric shapes to the tote bag. Follow the instructions on the Mod Podge Fabric bottle for curing and laundering.

Upcycled Drawer Shelves

Before beginning your project, be sure to read & familiarize yourself with the information on pages 2-5.

SHOPPING LIST

- ☐ Mod Podge® Ultra Matte Chalk
- ☐ FolkArt® Home Decor™ Chalk (Nautical & Spanish Moss)
- ☐ Assorted sports-themed scrapbook paper
- ☐ Assorted phrases & motifs cut from paper
- ☐ Wooden drawers (our drawers are 8½"h x 11"w x 4"d & 12½"w x 5h x 4"d)
- ☐ Sawtooth hangers (optional)
- ☐ Basic tools

To make each Shelf:

Always allow paint and Mod Podge to dry completely between applications.

1. Remove any hardware and prepare the drawer. Paint the drawer the desired color.

2. Turn the drawer on end so the drawer front becomes the top of the shelf.

3. Cut pieces of scrapbook paper to fit the inner sides of the drawer. Use Mod Podge to adhere the paper pieces to the inner sides. Use the squeegee or brayer to smooth the paper.

4. Cut the desired paper shapes and motifs from scrapbook paper.

5. Use Mod Podge to adhere the papers and motifs to the shelf back. Use the squeegee or brayer to smooth the paper. Apply 2-3 topcoats of Mod Podge over the entire shelf.

6. Replace the hardware. Add sawtooth hangers to the shelf back, if desired.

Doily Bowl

SHOPPING LIST

- ☐ Mod Podge® Stiffy®
- ☐ 10" diameter cotton doily
- ☐ 6" diameter glass bowl to shape doily
- ☐ Large zip-closure plastic bag
- ☐ Plastic wrap
- ☐ Tall jar

Before beginning your project, be sure to read & familiarize yourself with the information on pages 2-5.

To make the Bowl:

1. Cover your work surface and exterior of the bowl with plastic wrap. Place the jar on the plastic wrap and turn the bowl upside down on the jar to keep the doily from touching your work surface.

2. Place the doily in the bag and cover with Mod Podge Stiffy; close the bag. Squeeze the bag to completely coat the doily with Mod Podge Stiffy.

3. Remove the doily from the bag and drape over the glass bowl, smoothing the bottom so it is flat. Pinch, pleat, or fold the doily edges to give the desired shape to your bowl *(Photo 1)*. Allow the doily bowl to dry for about 12-24 hours; remove from the glass bowl.

Tin Can Bird Feeders

SHOPPING LIST

- ☐ Mod Podge® Outdoor
- ☐ 3 large recycled food cans
- ☐ Assorted floral scrapbook paper
- ☐ Jute (green & natural)
- ☐ Basic tools

Before beginning your project, be sure to read & familiarize yourself with the information on pages 2-5.

To make each Birdfeeder:

Always allow paint and Mod Podge to dry completely between applications.

1. Measure the height (not including the top/bottom rims) and circumference of your can. Add $1/2$" to the circumference measurement. Cut a piece of scrapbook paper this measurement. For the bottom, draw around the can on coordinating scrapbook paper; cut out the bottom circle just inside the drawn line.

2. Use Mod Podge to adhere the papers to the can. Apply 2-3 topcoats of Mod Podge to the entire can. Allow Mod Podge to dry for 72 hours before placing outside.

3. Leaving a tail the desired hanging length, wrap jute around the can 8-10 times. Tie a knot close to the can and then knot the loose ends together. Add a jute bow in a contrasting color.

Sparkle Jar

SHOPPING LIST _____

- ☐ Mod Podge® Matte
- ☐ Mod Podge® Sparkle
- ☐ FolkArt® Acrylic Paint (Italian Sage & Bark Brown)
- ☐ Purple quart-size canning jar with metal screw band
- ☐ 2½" wide strip of gold scrapbook paper

- ☐ 2 floral-themed rectangles cut from scrapbook paper (ours are 2¾" x 4¼")
- ☐ Coordinating tag (we used a 1½" x 2½" rectangular tag)
- ☐ Jute
- ☐ Soft cloth
- ☐ Basic tools

Before beginning your project, be sure to read & familiarize yourself with the information on pages 2-5.

To make the Jar:

Always allow paint and Mod Podge to dry completely between applications.

1. Measure the circumference of your jar. Cut a 2½" wide strip of gold scrapbook paper the diameter measurement, piecing if needed. Beginning and ending at the center back, use Mod Podge Matte to adhere the strip to the jar.

2. Use Mod Podge Matte to adhere a floral-themed rectangle to the jar front and the jar back.

3. Paint the screw band with Italian Sage. Pour out a small amount of Bark Brown and thin with a few drops of water. Apply a coat of thinned Bark Brown over the Italian Sage and wipe away the excess with a soft cloth.

4. Apply a topcoat of Mod Podge Sparkle to the entire jar and band.

5. Attach the tag with a jute bow.

Birthday Plate

SHOPPING LIST

- ☐ Mod Podge® Dishwasher Safe
- ☐ FolkArt® Multi-Surface Paint (Cayman Blue & Bark Brown)
- ☐ 3" high letter stencils
- ☐ 9" dia. clear glass flat-bottom plate
- ☐ 1 sheet **each** of 3 coordinating scrapbook papers
- ☐ Double-sided tape
- ☐ Basic tools

Before beginning your project, be sure to read & familiarize yourself with the information on pages 2-5.

To make the plate:
Always allow paint and Mod Podge to dry completely between applications and steps.

1. For the circles, cut an 8" dia. circle from one paper and a 6" dia. circle from a second paper.

2. For the numbers, place the stencil right side down on the wrong side of the third scrapbook paper and draw the desired numbers; cut out on drawn lines.

3. Using a dry brush loaded with a small amount of Bark Brown, accent all of the paper edges.

4. Layer the 8" circle, 6" circle, and then the numbers using small pieces of double-sided tape to secure the layers.

5. Apply a coat of Mod Podge to the front of the motif and to the back of the plate. Center the motif *under* the plate and press in place. Use the squeegee to smooth the paper.

6. Apply 2-3 topcoats of Mod Podge over the wrong side of the motif, being sure the paper edges are well covered. Refer to Mod Podge Dishwasher Safe instructions on the bottle for curing time.

7. Paint the entire plate back with Cayman Blue. Refer to the curing instructions located on the bottle.

Gift Bag

SHOPPING LIST

- ☐ Mod Podge® Paper Matte and Gloss
- ☐ Black paper gift bag (our bag measures 10$^{1}/_{2}$"h x 8"w x 4$^{3}/_{4}$"d)
- ☐ 8-10 assorted vintage-inspired scrapbook papers
- ☐ Ivory scrapbook paper
- ☐ Assorted motifs cut from paper (we used a bird, a butterfly, and a glitter swirl)
- ☐ Black paint pen
- ☐ 8" length of jute
- ☐ Gold flower button or charm (for paper flower center)
- ☐ 2$^{1}/_{2}$" circle punch
- ☐ 3" circle punch with scalloped edges
- ☐ Lace border punch
- ☐ Scalloped-edged scissors
- ☐ Wax paper
- ☐ Craft glue
- ☐ Basic tools

Before beginning your project, be sure to read & familiarize yourself with the information on pages 2-5.

To make the Gift Bag:

Always allow Mod Podge to dry completely between applications.

1. For the bag cover, measure across the long and short top edges of your bag and add 2$^{1}/_{2}$" to each measurement. Cut a rectangle of scrapbook paper this measurement. On the wrong side, draw a line 1$^{1}/_{4}$" from each edge. Make a cut at each corner where indicated by the blue lines in **Fig.1**.

Fig. 1

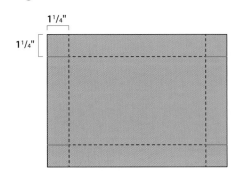

2. Cut 4 strips of ivory paper 2¹/₂"w x 10" (or 2" longer than your longest top edge measurement from Step 1 if using a larger bag). Follow the punch manufacturer's instructions to punch the lace design on the 4 strips. Trimming as needed, glue 1 strip to the wrong side of each flap.

3. Punch a 2¹/₂" circle from ivory paper and a 3" scalloped-edge circle from a contrasting color paper. Cut the desired motif from printed paper. Use Mod Podge Matte to adhere the circles and motif to the cover center.

4. Measure the bag as shown and mark the placement for the handle slits on the cover *(Figs. 2-3)*. Cut an ¹/₈" wide slit from mark to mark on each side of the cover.

Fig. 2

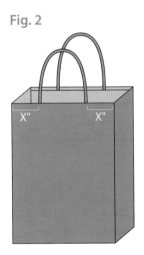

Fig. 3

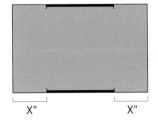

5. Fold the flaps to the wrong side along the drawn lines; overlap and glue flaps at the corners.

6. For the flower, coat the right side of a piece of scrapbook paper with Mod Podge Gloss. Use the patterns, page 31, to cut 4 large, 3 medium, and 3 small petals from the paper. Cut a ¹/₂" slit in the flat end of each petal.

7. Overlap the slit of 1 large petal to make the petal curl; glue in place. Repeat with the remaining petals. Overlapping as needed, glue the 4 large petals into a flower shape; repeat with the medium and small petals. Stack and glue the petals to make the flower. Glue the button to the center of the flower.

8. Use the leaf pattern, page 31, to cut 3 leaves from contrasting papers. Layer and glue the leaves, jute piece, and flower to the bag cover.

9. For the tag, cut a 5¹/₂" square from a print paper and a 5" and 3¹/₂" square each from contrasting solid papers. Trim across opposite sides of the 3¹/₂" square with scalloped-edged scissors. Use Mod Podge Matte to layer and adhere the squares together. Trimming as needed, adhere the glitter swirl and bird to the tag. Use the paint pen to write a sentiment on the tag. Adhere the tag to the bag front with Mod Podge.

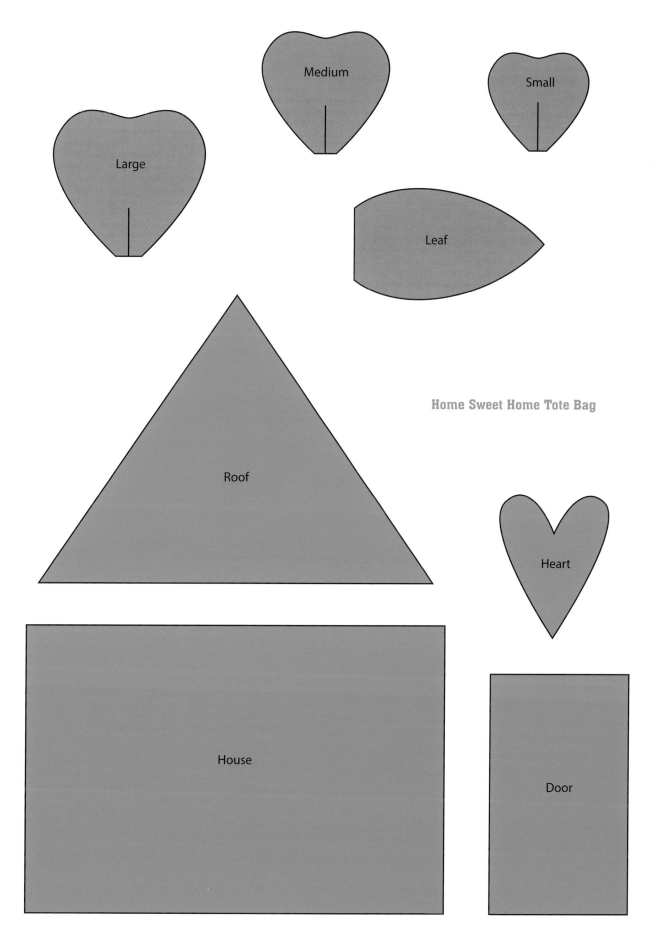

Medium

Small

Large

Leaf

Roof

Home Sweet Home Tote Bag

Heart

House

Door

PLAID® is a registered trademark of Plaid Enterprises, Inc., Norcross, Georgia. Used with express permission. All rights reserved.
To purchase products and see more project ideas, visit www.plaidonline.com

Copyright © 2015 by Leisure Arts, Inc., 104 Champs Blvd., STE 100, Maumelle, AR 72113-6738. All rights reserved. This publication is protected under federal copyright laws. Reproduction or distribution of this publication or any other Leisure Arts publication, including publications which are out of print, is prohibited unless specifically authorized. This includes, but is not limited to, any form of reproduction or distribution on or through the Internet, including posting, scanning, or e-mail transmission.

We have made every effort to ensure that these instructions are accurate and complete. We cannot, however, be responsible for human error, typographical mistakes, or variations in individual work.

Leisure Arts Production Team: Technical Writer – Jean Lewis; Technical Associate – Frances Huddleston and Mary Sullivan Hutcheson; Editorial Writer – Susan Frantz Wiles; Senior Graphic Artist – Lora Puls; Graphic Artist – Cailen Cochran; Photo Stylist – Sondra Daniel; Photographer – Ken West.

Plaid Enterprises Production Team: Category Director – Andrea Henfield; Brand Manager – Connie Lanham; Creative Director – Paul LaPlaca; Design Director – Jackie Wynia; Communications Director – Jon Bogle; Communications Manager – Rena Williams; Contributing Designers – Julie Lewis, Sherri Ragsdale, Kirsten Jones, and Karen Reif.